OFFICE
OF THE
SURREY
INDEPENDENT

WIMBLEDON
PAST & PRESENT

Wimbledon Stadium, Plough Lane, 1938. The stadium was opened in 1928 for greyhound races and motorcycle speedway racing. Stock-car racing was introduced later.

An aerial view of Wimbledon town and railway station, *c.* 1925. The road bridge over the railway tracks at the station is prominent. St George's Road is at the bottom left and the Broadway runs from bottom left to top right.

WIMBLEDON
PAST & PRESENT

PATRICK LOOBEY

WHSmith

First published in the United Kingdom in 2002 by
Sutton Publishing Limited exclusively for
WHSmith, Greenbridge Road, Swindon SN3 3LD

British Library Cataloguing in Publication Data
A catalogue record for this book is available from the British Library.

ISBN 0-7509-3115-9

Illustrations

Front endpaper: The Broadway, 1907.
Back endpaper: The Broadway, 2002.
Half title page: Wimbledon Theatre, *c.* 1914.
Title page: A touching scene in South Park Gardens, Trinity Road, *c.* 1912.

The Lover's Walk, Wimbledon Hill, *c.* 1912.

Typeset in 11/14pt Photina and produced by
Sutton Publishing Limited, Phoenix Mill,
Thrupp, Stroud, Gloucestershire GL5 2BU.
Printed and bound in England by
J.H. Haynes & Co. Ltd, Sparkford.

Contents

High Street, Merton, and the River Wandle, *c.* 1922. The original two-bay entrance (centre) to the London General Omnibus Co. bus garage was built in 1913 and later enlarged to three bays (see p. 114). To the left is the King's Head public house which claims a founding date of 1496.

St Mary's, Wimbledon parish church, *c.* 1912.

Introduction

The name of Wimbledon will conjure up in many people's minds the sport of tennis and possibly the Common. Wimbledon can be justly proud of both, but the area has much more to offer than having its name tagged on to one sport. Wimbledon Park is an oasis among the urban sprawl and the area can boast four golf courses, and horse-riding schools are still in operation. The varied architecture ranges from the seventeenth century right through to modern tower blocks – thankfully not too many. The many old pubs attract a steady stream of visitors as do the various retail establishments.

The story of modern Wimbledon commenced with the opening of the railway station in 1838; additional platforms were required in 1855 for the London, Brighton & South Coast Railway and in 1889 for the District Railway. The introduction of trams in 1907 gave people the mobility to explore neighbouring areas and was to bring more business to the town. What was an expanding village of 4,644 people in 1861 had increased its population to 55,000 by 1911, with an attendant growth in shopping facilities, churches, libraries, schools, public houses and so on, and in the twentieth century a theatre and several cinemas were added.

Merton Park level crossing, Kingston Road, 1907. On the left is the sign for the White Hart public house and next to the crossing is the railway signal-box, later removed.

The village has remained largely untouched by the modern movement for renewal, unlike the town centre where in the 1980s and 1990s Worple Road, Hill Road and the Broadway had over-large blocks imposed on them and the former Town Hall was transformed into a retail emporium. Many of the large mid-Victorian mansions, at the end of their hundred-year leases, have been replaced by small blocks of flats but many, with their individual style of architecture, have survived to enhance the leafy streets.

Wimbledon was forcibly amalgamated into the new London Borough of Merton in 1965 but the local population still consider themselves as of this town and not of Merton, and most believe fervently in Wimbledon's separate identity.

The photographs in this book have been selected to compare early twentieth-century views of Wimbledon with those we can enjoy today. Every effort was made to duplicate the views from the same vantage point, but modern Wimbledon abounds with an excess of road signs and street furniture, and with the growth of modern traffic and the need for pedestrian barriers it seemed wisest to obtain the modern photographs from the nearest practical position. Sometimes parked vehicles and trees also necessitated a slight alteration in viewpoint. The camera lenses used in the past were different from those available today and much use of wide-angle lenses is evident in the old photographs. All the modern views were taken over several days in mid-June 2002 when the trees were in full bloom, and many of the streetscapes and buildings are therefore obscured by foliage.

All the photographs in this book are from the collection of Patrick Loobey. Copies are available from him at 231 Mitcham Lane, Streatham, London, SW16 6PY. Tel: 020 8769 0072; email: pat@loobey.co.uk; website: www.loobey.co.uk

The River Wandle, High Street, Merton, 1907. The vacant property to the right of the King's Head public house was soon to be sold to the London General Omnibus Co.

The Town Centre

Joseph Ely founded his drapery store near the railway station in 1876 and opened this store, on the corner of Worple Road, in 1886. The store-front was remodelled with a rounded corner in 1906/7 to accommodate the arrival of the electric tramway system. The store was rebuilt in 1986 (*see* p. 18).

Hill Road, *c.* 1910 and 2002. Alwyn Road is to the right. On the right are the offices of Robert John Thompson FRIBA, architect, and beyond, the premises of his father, Davis Stewart Thompson & Sons, nurserymen. The nursery was soon to be built over with a parade of modest shops and a block of offices is presently replacing these. The 1880s shopping parade on the left corner of Mansel Road was demolished and rebuilt in about 1994 and is now undergoing cleaning behind the plastic sheeting and scaffolding.

Hill Road, *c.* 1914 and 2002. The bank on the corner of Compton Road (right) has been converted into a bar named All-Bar-One. The parade of shops on the left once contained family-owned establishments but now has a Health Zone, a health food shop, a branch of the Nationwide Building Society and several bars and cafés.

Hill Road from the corner of Woodside Road, *c.* 1933 and 2002. The motor showroom on the left is advertising Armstrong Siddeleys – a marque no longer available. The three-storey buildings on the left have been demolished and are being replaced by an office block. The tram tracks on Hill Road had been closed in December 1932 and the terminus was cut back to outside the Town Hall, leaving motor traffic free to park on the hill.

Hill Road, 1907 and 2002. The one part of Wimbledon that has not suffered the developers' touch in recent years is on Hill Road from Bank Buildings, on the corner of Compton Road, as far down as Alexandra Road. The library was built in 1886–7 and opened in 1887; it was enlarged in 1902 and further alterations and improvements took place in 1995. The low wall and railings have been removed and the pavement extended outside the library. The Alexandra public house dates from 1876. The first floor has been rebuilt outwards towards the roadway since the early photograph was taken.

Hill Road at the corner of Worple Road, *c.* 1912 and 2002. Ely's department store still occupies the same corner position but was rebuilt in 1986 in an anonymous glass and aluminium style. The centre of Wimbledon has been altered dramatically throughout the 1990s with several oversize developments, such as that beyond Ely's store which has plunged the lower end of Hill Road into permanent shade.

Hill Road, *c.* 1910 and 2002. Ely's may have been totally rebuilt but Ryman's stationer's still retains its original 1860s first floor house frontage. The National Westminster Bank premises on the corner of St George's Road were built in 1995.

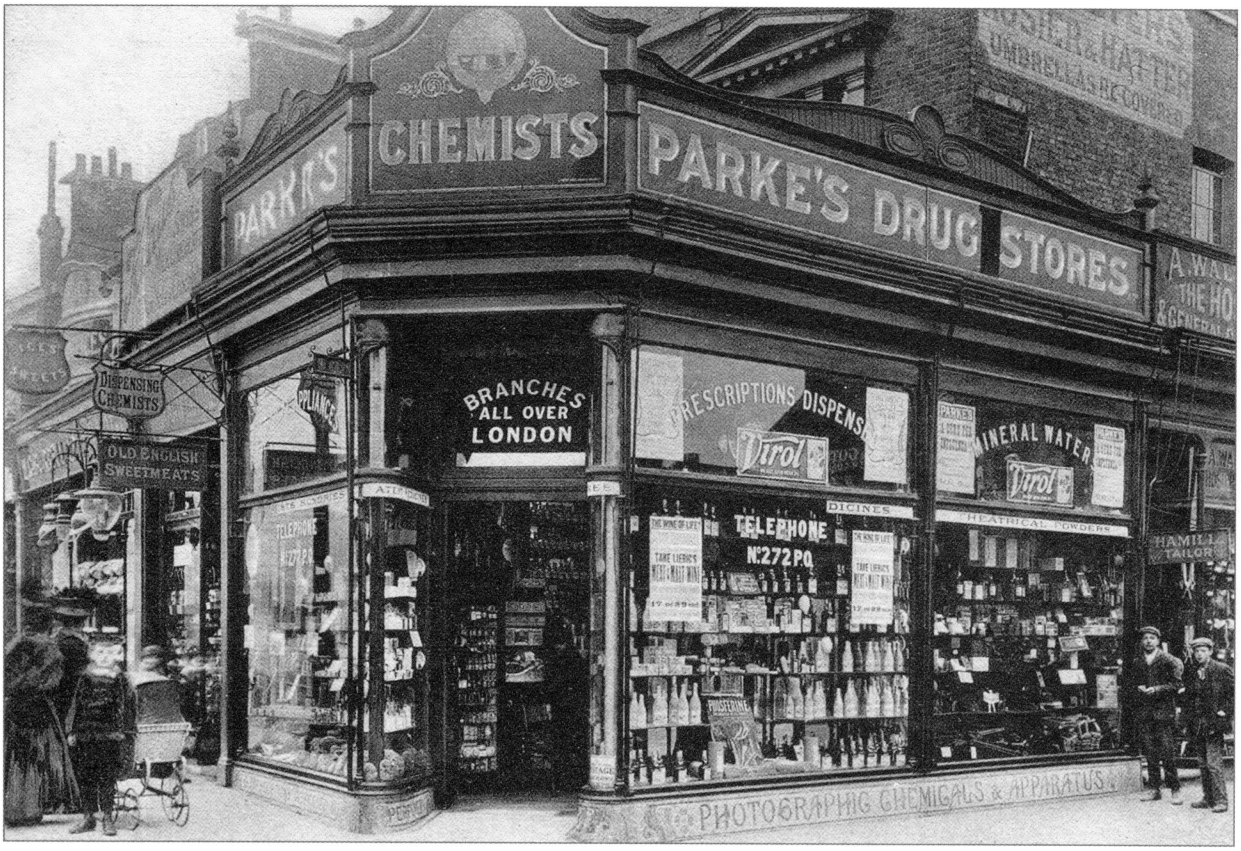

Parke's drug stores, 14 Hill Road, *c.* 1906. The store was part of a chain spread across London that supplied proprietary medicines and their own brands of cures. One of them was Parke's own 'Cure for Exhaustion'; also advertised was Liebig's Meat and Malt wine at 1*s* 7*d* and 2*s* 9*d* per bottle. One small change from today's arrangements with any pharmacy is that they would send a messenger to fetch a prescription after receiving a telephone call to Wimbledon 272 and would then deliver it. Starbucks coffee house now occupies the corner of St George's Road and Hill Road.

Hill Road, *c.* 1926 and 2002. The 1860s houses on the left, at the lower end of Hill Road, and the 1870s shops on the right near the station entrance were to survive into the 1980s when redevelopment of Wimbledon's centre took place. The only recognisable structure in the 2002 view is the premises on the corner of Worple Road, now taken by Haart estate agents. Notice the sign for Parke's drug store hanging from the second floor on the left in the earlier view.

The long-awaited trams finally arrived in Wimbledon in 1907, when this photograph was taken. The tram is crossing the recently widened bridge over the railway lines next to Wimbledon station. To the right of the tram can be seen the bridge wall, leaving an open aspect along the railway. The bridge had a small two-storey parade of shops added in the 1930s but these were demolished and replaced in the early 1990s with a white-clad three-storey block that fronts Wimbledon Bridge House at 1 Hartfield Road. In the background is the Prince of Wales public house, built in about 1870.

Wimbledon station, *c.* 1912 and 2002. In 1912 it had an air about it of a country halt with cabs and private broughams awaiting their passengers. The station was built in 1838 for the London, Brighton & South Coast Railway and enlarged in 1889 when the District Railway first arrived. The Southern Railway Co. built the present station entrance in 1929. The forecourt was redesigned recently and taxicabs now wait down to the left of the station.

The Broadway, 1907 and 2002. One of the newly introduced trams is negotiating the bridge at the station at the permitted speed of 8 mph. Hartfield Road is to the left. It is no wonder that the Wimbledon Society has described the early 1990s new building, containing W.H. Smith's and Waterstones bookshop, as the 'Fridge on the Bridge'.

The Broadway, *c.* 1914 and 2002. It had yet to see the rebuilding of the Town Hall and still sported a variety of advertising signs above the shops on the corner of Queens Road. To the left is the commercial entrance to the station where a number of coal merchants and builders merchants conducted their operations. The 2002 scene appears to be a clutter of signs, traffic lights and pedestrian islands in the roadway, all required to control the recently introduced one-way traffic system that runs for about 200 yards along the Broadway.

Barclays Bank now occupies the premises of the London & Provincial Bank back in 1907, although the building frontage looks unaltered. A single-decker bus was chosen for the modern scene, as a modern double-decker bus would have overwhelmed the view. The addition of the railings on the kerbside has not enhanced the general scene very much but is there to protect pedestrians and prevent them from crossing the road away from the designated light-controlled crossings.

The earlier Town Hall, seen here in about 1914, was built in 1878 as administrative offices for the local Board of Health. It became the Town Hall in 1905 when Wimbledon gained its borough charter. Rebuilt and enlarged, the new Town Hall opened in November 1931 and remained the administrative centre of Wimbledon until 1983 when all the municipal staff were relocated to Crown House in Morden. The building was reused in the early 1990s as part of the Centre Court shopping development and the entrance porch now sports a sign for a Tesco Metro store.

The Town Hall, pictured soon after the rebuilding in 1931. The people of the town were – and are – proud of their heritage and many functions were held here to honour local heroes, the wildest greeting being reserved for Wimbledon Football Club, in the first division since 1986, who in 1988 brought home the FA Cup. The Civic Hall attached to the Town Hall was then still in use but was soon demolished to make way for the new entrance to the Centre Court shopping development.

The Town Hall in about 1933, with a London-bound tram waiting on the terminus. After the Wimbledon Hill route was abandoned in December 1932, a scissors cross-over was installed outside the Town Hall to enable the trams to reverse towards London. The other overhead wires were for the trolleybuses. The modern view of the former Town Hall is obscured by trees planted since the opening of Centre Court, whose main entrance is to the left (*see* page 31).

A London Council Tramways car advertising Black & White whisky is at the terminus on the left while one of its new competitors pulls up outside the Town Hall. The trolleybuses were introduced in 1931 and were known in the transport world as 'Diddlers'. The last trolleybus from Wimbledon ran in 1962. The recently planted trees and pedestrian barrier certainly make it difficult to copy the earlier scene, and no. 57 buses now perform the duties of the old trolleybuses and trams.

The Town Hall, *c.* 1933 and 2002. The old photograph was taken from Victoria Crescent, which has recently been subsumed into the entrance of a new retail and leisure complex on the Broadway called the Crescent, to be opened in 2002. The rotunda to the left of the former Town Hall covers the main entrance to the Centre Court shopping area.

The Broadway in 1907 only had horse-drawn traffic and the electric trams to fill the roadway. The trams were only 7ft 2in wide while the modern bus takes up 8ft 2½in of road space. By some design fluke the new entrance to the Crescent shopping centre, beyond the bus, has a cupola similar to that on the earlier corner roof, seen beyond the horse and cart.

The Broadway, 1907 and 2002. The diesel-powered van has taken over from the horse-drawn delivery cart (whose only fuel requirements were water and hay plus some oats) and the pollution-free electric tram has been superseded by the diesel-engined bus. On the left in June 2002 work is taking place to complete the extension to the Safeway supermarket and also the new entrance to the Crescent shopping centre.

F.W. Woolworth's store (left) has occupied the corner of Gladstone Road since 1935 but like many stores in the Broadway it has been 'modernised' and rebuilt. The white stone-fronted building, further along on the left, is the new Safeway supermarket that stretches southwards to the newly extended Hartfield Road. The young man on the right in the 1907 scene is pulling a barrow covered with advertisements for a sale at some local establishment.

Wimbledon Theatre, *c.* 1914 and 2001. Wimbledon Theatre was opened on Boxing Day 1910 with a pantomime, *Jack and Jill*. The theatre is especially popular for its annual productions of pantomimes that still draw a good audience each Christmas. Many West End plays are first performed at Wimbledon, no doubt because of its large stage area.

The Broadway in 1907. The theatre would not be built for another three years and two large houses occupy its site on the corner of Russell Road. The tall building on the corner of Palmerston Road (beyond the tram) was Holy Trinity School. Kings Road is on the left.

The Broadway, 1907 and 2002. In the 1907 scene children can be seen playing in the front playground of Holy Trinity School. The shops on the right have since been rebuilt with three storeys of flats above. The cobblestones at the entrance to J.T. Noakes' carriage and cab booking office and yard has managed to survive but the buildings were long since demolished.

Holy Trinity School was converted into the Kings Palace cinema, with 400 seats, in 1910. The foyer was built over the former playground. The old school also had enough space to accommodate a Temperance billiard and snooker hall and in the 1920s it even housed a roller-skating rink. The cinema closed on 30 April 1955 but the building remained in use as a shopping arcade until demolition in 1993–4. As part of the over-grand development plans for Wimbledon it was demolished. Ten years later the site remains empty and only in use as a car park.

Holy Trinity Church was built in 1862 on the Broadway, although until the early 1930s this stretch of roadway was still known as Merton Road. The church today is almost hidden by the trees. Beyond the trees in the modern view can be seen the Polka Children's Theatre, which opened in 1979.

The junction of Merton Road and the Broadway, 1907 and 2002. The corner shop on the right, occupied by Mann, Crossman & Paulin's off-licence, is still an off-licence, known today as Broadway Wines. One sad aspect of today's streetscape is the preponderance of ugly steel shutters covering the shopfronts, as seen on the premises on the left.

An LCC route no. 2 tram, pictured heading towards Wimbledon along Merton Road in about 1934, has just entered the single-track part of this narrow section of road. Traffic lights for the trams were installed in 1940 at the corner of Latimer Road and also on the corner of Pelham Road. These tram traffic lights survived until the removal of the LCC tramway system in 1951.

A modern no. 57 bus now negotiates the heavy traffic as it turns out of Merton High Street into Merton Road – where in 1907 the tram had no competition in its journey toward Tooting. The Grove Hotel (right) was rebuilt in 1912 and renamed the Grove Tavern on reopening. The Horse and Groom public house in the High Street was not involved in the rebuilding of this corner to make way for the extension of the City & South London Railway Co., which resulted in the opening of South Wimbledon Underground station in September 1926.

Wimbledon Streets

Wimbledon fire station, pictured about five years after it opened in 1904. This replaced the smaller station in the High Street opposite the Dog and Fox public house. Motor fire appliances replaced the horse-drawn steam engines in 1913. The town centre development plans saw the station close in the late 1980s and the fire brigade moved to new premises on Kingston Road, Merton. The Queens Road station was saved after much campaigning and now survives as part of the Centre Court shopping development.

Arthur Road hill still had some plots of land left for house building in about 1910, as seen by the empty spaces on both sides of the road. The modern vista includes the distant high-rise office blocks at Canary Wharf to the east of the City of London.

Wimbledon Park station was opened in 1889 by the London & South Western Railway Company as a new feeder route for the District Railway to Wimbledon from the West End of London. The station was handed over to London Underground in 1984 but the track and signals are still maintained by Railtrack. Work is under way in June 2002 to pile and shore up the embankment on the Up track on the left.

Arthur Road and Wimbledon Park station in 1907. The estate agents' offices of Ryan and Penfold (right) were responsible for much of the house building and development in the immediate area at this time. The pavement outside the station has been relaid many times but an odd survivor is a granite stone sett by the entrance, bearing the brass numbers 26. This was the local council licence number for a newspaper vendor's sales pitch that has not been in use for probably at least fifty years.

Arthur Road, 1912 and 2002. The post office is still serving the local community but Mussel & Son are no longer the proprietors. The bank on the corner of Melrose Avenue is now the office of Kinleigh, Folkhard & Hayward, estate agents.

Alverstone Avenue, 1914 and 2002. In 1914 it had just the two street lamps to boast of, the one on the right and another on the corner of Ashen Grove. The cast-iron railings on the garden walls were removed in 1940/1 to help with the wartime scrap drive. The cast iron was graded and put to use in armament manufacture where strength was not a requirement.

Ashen Grove, *c.* 1914 and 2002. Braemar Avenue is on the left. The original roofs were of Welsh slate but these have mistakenly been replaced with tiles during the 1970s and up to the present day.

Birkbeck Road, *c.* 1914 and 2002. The only traffic is a horse-drawn bread van making deliveries, and the children can play happily in the street. In the distance is Queens Road and to the left is Faraday Road.

Burleigh Road, *c.* 1912 and 2002. In 1912 wooden fencing was deemed sufficient to denote a property boundary rather than the brick walls that appear to have sprung up within recent years. Another sign of modern times is the need to restrain commuters from parking their cars all day long in the vicinity.

Crooked Billet, *c*. 1914 and 2002. On a sunny day in June 2002 people are spread out across the green of Crooked Billet, in place of the washing line seen in the earlier view. The former shops on the right have been transformed into living accommodation. The Hand in Hand public house stands to the right of the cars and the Crooked Billet public house is the taller building beyond the trees.

Dryden Road, looking down from Haydens Road, *c.* 1914 and 2002. The children appear to have the road to themselves to use as a playground. The view across the River Wandle towards the Grove Hospital, Tooting (now St George's), has since been blocked by the construction of Garfield Road at the eastern end of Dryden Road.

Gap Road has been renamed several times. In the middle of the nineteenth century it was called Garratt Road and later Cemetery Road. Understandably, as development took place, the residents opted for an alternative to the Cemetery Road. The 1912 view includes the Wimbledon Isolation Hospital. Covering 5 acres, it was opened in 1900 with space for eighty-two beds. When it was demolished, the Poplar Court housing estate was erected on the site, retaining the original wall and railings from the hospital.

Gordondale Road, 1912 and 2002. In the 1912 view only a horse-drawn coal cart and a small hand-pushed milk delivery cart are to be seen, leaving plenty of space to view the factories and schools of Earlsfield on the far side of the River Wandle. The houses of Lucien Road now block the earlier view and the road is full of vehicles.

Grange Road in 1913 still had its wooden fencing but little of it survives; just as in Burleigh Road such fences have largely been replaced with brick walls.

Haydons Road, 1910 and 2002. The Station Stores, selling Charrington's Ales in 1910, is now the Haydons off-licence. This small row of shops lies between Tennyson Road and Dryden Road. This area of Wimbledon has hardly changed over the decades, the only major difference being the addition of roof loft extensions to some of the houses.

The tram in Haydons Road is en route to Summerstown via Plough Lane in 1907. There are two major changes in these views: the properties on the corner of Haydon Park Road were bombed in the Second World War and have been replaced by a petrol station and a small block of flats, and the absence of sun awnings to cover the shop-fronts.

This row of shops in Haydons Road lies between North Road and Cowper Road. The parade of shopping outlets appears busy and of interest back in 1912 but it all has a look of dereliction today. Three of the shops have been converted into houses. It's strange how confectionery shops almost always had a small group of children standing outside them in old photographs!

Hartfield Road in 1914 had a range of outlets to invite trade of all interests. The ironmongers S.R. Love & Sons at no. 7 (right) were in business for many years supplying the local area with its locks, nails, paint, and so on. Over-large office blocks have been built within the past ten years on the corner of Hartfield Crescent on the right, producing the shadows seen here. One small terrace of original shops survives between Graham Road and Beulah Road, further along on the right.

Home Park Road in about 1912 offered a grand vista of Wimbledon Park and the golf course. The railing has since been replaced with a concrete panel fence and the trees have grown to enormous size. Further along on the right can be seen the few acres sold off by the borough council for development in 1925 to defray the costs of opening the public park at the north-east corner of Wimbledon Park. The council had bought 150 acres from the Spencer family in 1913 to prevent building development on the north-eastern part of Wimbledon Park.

After the District Railway was opened in 1889 the southern part of the Wimbledon Park Estate was developed at great pace. Kenilworth Avenue was built soon after and is seen above in about 1912.

Kenilworth Avenue, near the corner of Landgrove Road, *c.* 1914 and 2002. The two large chimneys in the distance were part of Durnsford Road power station, which provided electricity to the railway companies. It should not to be confused with the municipal power station, which stood on Durnsford Road where the Homebase DIY store is now situated.

Landgrove Road, *c.* 1914 and 2002. In the old photograph the isolation hospital in Gap Road can be seen beyond Strathhearne Road and the railway cutting. The Poplar Court housing estate can just be glimpsed through the trees in the later view.

Leopold Road, at the corner with Bernard Gardens, 1912 and 2002. The sandstone window openings on the buildings on the left have all been painted to help preserve them from weathering. The road was named after Queen Victoria's fourth son, Leopold, Duke of Albany (1853–84).

The observant eye will notice that a few of the cast-iron ornamental finials have survived on the rooftop parapets of the shops in Leopold Road. The parade would have been fairly new and the paint still bright and glossy in the 1906 view. The outlets here today can boast more variety and individuality than many other shopping parades, possibly because they do not belong to any nationwide chains of stores.

Woodside parade of shops, Leopold Road, 1912 and 2002 – ninety years later the real change is in the amount of private transport in use. The outfitters' shop on the right-hand corner had been built since the 1906 view (*see* opposite). Thankfully a few of the early ornate lampposts survive in Gap Road.

This road was named Marlborough Road when Mussel & Son, who ran the post office in Arthur Road, published this postcard in about 1910 but it has since been renamed Stroud Road. Melrose Avenue is at the far end. The milkman was from the Wimbledon Park Farm Dairy in Revelstoke Road.

Normanton Avenue, *c.* 1914 and 2002. St Luke's Church, Farquhar Road is in the distance. The road was developed between 1896 and 1901 as part of Clonmore Road in Southfields but this section was renamed Normanton Road in 1906. The trees have not become so overgrown as to hide the modern view of the church.

One of the newly introduced trams in Plough Lane en route for the Summerstown terminus in 1907. The plot of land to the left was home to Wimbledon Football Club from 1910 until the 1990s when the ground was deemed more valuable for development than for playing football. The team, having won the FA Cup at Wembley in 1988, has since played at other team's grounds and appears somewhat detached from its home supporters. Several epitaphs and messages (including a tombstone) were left at the old entrance to the ground by heartbroken fans. Latest news is that the club's home base will be in Milton Keynes, Buckinghamshire.

The view down Queens Road from Haydons Road, *c*. 1912 and 2002. In the distance can be seen Queens Road School on the corner of Craven Gardens. It is now called Priory Church of England primary school.

As part of the Centre Court shopping development it was proposed in the early 1990s to demolish the Baptist Church, built in 1897 to seat a thousand people, together with the Magistrates Court and the fire station in Queens Road, seen above in about 1910. These buildings were saved from the demolitioner's ball and the church is now a Boots pharmacy and an extension to the shopping centre. On the right is the police station on the corner of South Park Road.

Part of the planning and development schemes for Wimbledon dreamt up in the 1980s involved blocking access to the Broadway for traffic coming from Queens Road, and access is now only available to and from the Centre Court shopping centre. Traffic has been diverted along Trinity Road – much to the residents' annoyance. Traffic lights have mushroomed within the town centre and the view of Queen's Road from about 1910 is difficult to reproduce. Collins & Kew, booksellers, held a children's book sale each Monday, and a complete set of false teeth were available from Davies for 1*s* 1*d*.

This Edwardian view of St George's Road would have been easily recognisable in the early 1980s but it has changed enormously with the rebuilding of the heart of Wimbledon in the 1980s and 1990s. All four corners at the junction with Hill Road have been rebuilt. The tram shown here was en route to Hampton Court, a popular weekend destination for day trips.

St George's Road in 1912 had a good range of shopping outlets, a church, the army drill hall and accommodation. The enlarged Ely's store now has a presence here while the combined churches of Wimbledon have built the Sir Cyril Black Community Centre in the two-storey structure on the left. The two office blocks on the left run right through from Worple Road.

The original caption on this early photograph, of about 1910, states that it is Somerset Road but this stretch of road, north from Marryat Road, is now called Burghley Road.

Wimbledon might be blessed in having two large areas of parkland, in Wimbledon Common and also Wimbledon Park, but it has very few other parks; the one exception is South Park, Trinity Road, seen here in about 1920. On Sunday 16 June 2002 the recently formed Friends of South Park held a barbecue in aid of the park, to help save it from municipal indifference and lack of maintenance.

South Park in 1907 and 2002. The drinking fountain was donated by the Metropolitan Drinking Fountain & Cattle Trough Association. The urn has long since disappeared from the fountain but the Friends of South Park are hoping to win lottery funding to reinstate former features of the park that have either been removed or have been allowed to deteriorate. The park once had eight full-time staff to look after the flower-beds, grass, bandstand, fences, trees and pathways but the modern horticultural and maintenance management has been reduced to a bare minimum.

Mussel & Son's at the post office in Arthur Road were responsible for producing a series of postcard views of nearby streets in about 1910. They described this view as Stuart Road but it is in fact a view of Stroud Road from the corner of Melrose Avenue. A quick check of the window design and the marble columns near the entrance bears this out.

The first floor of the Alexandra public house in Hill Road was enlarged in 1925–7 and that is why the modern roofline appears so different from the 1907 view. The tram is about to leave for Hampton Court. A single-decker bus was chosen for today's view in Worple Road, as anything larger would have obscured the streetscape. A medieval term, 'worple' means the track, road or headland between ploughed fields.

Enough buildings have survived into the twenty-first century in Worple Road for us to get our bearings and recognise the scene. The photograph was taken soon after the roof was built on to tram no. 285 in 1910 or 1911. On the left is Worple Hall, which contained a roller-skating rink and shops, where 'animated pictures' were shown in 1906, before any purpose-built cinemas came to Wimbledon. Sainsbury's supermarket now occupies the site of the hairdressers and barber's shop on the right.

Worple Road, viewed from the junction with Pepys Road, *c.* 1910 and 2002. The slightly larger houses on the right were some of the first to be built in the 1890s on the new roadway extension to Worple Road. In the 1880s the road ended at Arterberry Road and the connection to Pepys Road and Raynes Park was not opened until 1891. The tram route was opened in 1907.

Wimbledon Buildings

A festival of song and dance is being promoted at Wimbledon Theatre in about 1914. The owner and manager, J.L. Mulholland, opened the theatre designed by Cecil Masey and Roy Young in 1910. The theatre had its own electricity generating plant to ensure supplies during performances. When so many theatres were disappearing throughout the 1970s and 1980s, it was heartening to see the numbers of patrons attending a variety of performances here.

Christ Church in Alwyne Road, *c.* 1910. The church has now been demolished and in its place have risen Central House, a four-storey office block, and Gladesbury Court, three-storey apartments with offices behind.

The Woodman public house, built in 1898, viewed from Durnsford Road railway bridge, *c.* 1914 and 2002. Minor alterations have included the addition of a conservatory and a patio drinking area on the south side of the pub, otherwise little has changed in the intervening years except that buses no longer use the pub as a terminus, just as a bus stop.

The Fox and Grapes public house on Camp Road in 1908 looks almost the same as it does today, except for the addition of some flower baskets and the removal of the pavement pub sign to a bracket attached to the building.

King's College School, Southside, *c.* 1912 and 2002. The school was founded in the Strand and moved to Wimbledon in 1897, occupying an eighteenth-century house called South Hayes, which had been a boys' school for a few years after 1811. The architect Sir Banister Fletcher designed the hall. King's College School is now regarded as one of England's better public schools with many pupils going on to attend university. In the modern view we can see that the school has been enlarged with the addition of extra classrooms. The postbox in front of the school hall has been moved about 30 yards to the right.

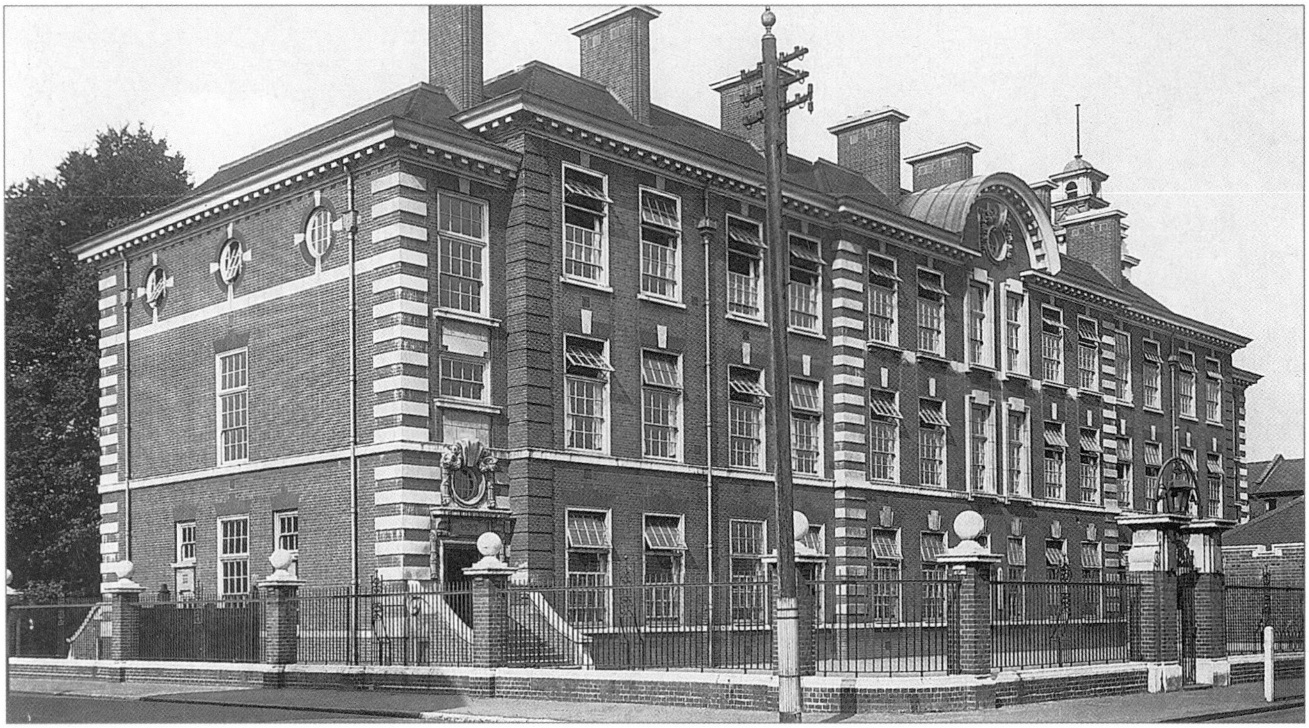

Pelham Road School was designed to accommodate 352 boys, 352 girls and 362 infants. The school building, seen here in about 1912, has now been sold off and converted into apartments called Downings House at 21 Southey Road. The former playground has had luxury flats, knows as the Pelhams, built on it. A new Pelham Primary School has been opened further to the south of both these buildings.

The All England Lawn Tennis and Croquet Club moved from Worple Road to Wimbledon Park in time to host the 1922 tournament, and is pictured here shortly after the new centre court had been built. The tournaments, held in June and July each year, are watched by a world-wide audience and queues to get in stretch for hundreds of yards all around the local streets. The water tower was built in 1922 and was supplied with water from the lake in the park opposite, but it is now connected to the water mains. The original plan was to have a clock face on its four sides, but this was never carried out.

Worple Road, *c.* 1938 and 2002. The Congregational Church, dating from 1884, was destroyed during the Second World War. The replacement building was erected as headquarters for the General, Municipal & Boilermakers Union and was called the GMB building. The Odeon cinema was opened on 20 April 1936 with 1,501 seats. The last film was shown there on 20 November 1960 and the building was subsequently demolished. The site of the old cinema now houses a seven-storey block containing a Lidl supermarket. The small shops on the left have been demolished to make way for the enlargement of Ely's store and the construction of a Sainsbury's supermarket.

The old post office at 1 Compton Road, seen here in about 1920, is now an English language school for Spanish-speaking pupils. Next door, Aldington House offices have been erected on the site of a congregational church. To the right, Marlborough Hall has been built to the rear of the library.

The council offices, 116–118 Kingston Road, *c.* 1912 and 2002. Merton Parish Council built the offices in 1900. In 1907 Merton Urban District Council came into being and the building became the local Town Hall. Attached was the Merton UDC fire station, seen to the left. A recent housing development has created Horatio Place, erected on the former storeyard of the council offices. The old building is still under Merton Council management.

Merton Park railway station was opened in 1868 as Lower Merton but the local landowner, John Innes, persuaded the railway company to alter the name in 1877. The station, seen here in about 1910, became redundant in the 1980s and a new housing scheme, Abbey Gardens, consisting of fourteen 2- and 3-bedroom houses, has been built on the former station forecourt. The new houses will be ready for ownership in the summer of 2002. The former booking office has also been converted into living accommodation and will be known as Old Station House.

Wimbledon Park Golf Club was founded in 1898, and the architect of the course was Willie Herbert jnr. The old clubhouse was destroyed by a flying bomb in 1944. The first tee is right outside the new clubhouse. The course has eighteen holes and the full distance is 3 miles. The course is leased from the All England Lawn Tennis and Croquet Club.

In 1907 Church Road was still part of Wimbledon Park Road. In the distance through the trees can be seen the lake in Wimbledon Park. The photograph was taken near the corner of Somerset Road, facing north. After the First World War the new Wimbledon Tennis grounds were built upon the open fields to the left, opening in 1922.

The pavement area on Hill Road just above Woodside, with children enjoying the railing-enclosed seats, in 1912. The small hut behind the children is where the trace horse was based. A trace horse, always called Jack, was in use from 1908 until just before the Second World War, to assist other horse-drawn traffic up the steep hill.

Wimbledon Common & Wimbledon Village

The windmill on Wimbledon Common was built in 1817 and stopped grinding corn in 1864. The mill was the headquarters of the National Rifle Association, whose meetings took place on the common from 1860 to 1889, when they moved the shoots to Bisley in Surrey. Lord Baden-Powell wrote *Scouting for Boys* here in 1907–8. The windmill was repaired in the 1970s and in 1976 the Windmill Museum was opened to explain the history, machinery and historical importance of windmills to local communities.

The banks of Rushmere Pond on Wimbledon Common before the First World War were always worn bare by the hordes of tiny feet paddling in the water. The pond has recently been allowed to become overgrown at the edges, with reeds obscuring the outlines of the water.

The small pond on Wimbledon Parkside, opposite Inner Park Road, in 1912 and 2002. There used to be a pathway through the water to allow small carts to enter to expand the wooden members of their wheels in dry weather. The pond is now an important wildlife reserve with moorhens and other aquatic birds enjoying their freedom. The large private dwellings in the background, Richmond House and Tyndale House, were demolished in the 1940s and 1950s and local authority housing erected in their place.

Caesar's Well, north of the golf course on Wimbledon Common, is fed from a natural spring. The water no longer appears from the well but from a pipe a few yards distant. The granite wall was installed in 1872 by Sir Henry Peek MP and the pine trees were planted soon after. The well is difficult to find as it seldom appears on any map.

Southside, Wimbledon Common, viewed from the High Street, *c.* 1920 and 2002. Lingfield Road is to the left.

West Place, Wimbledon Common, *c.* 1912 and 2002. Two hire carriages wait outside H. Dormer's Job Master's office on the corner of Camp Road. In keeping with the increasing mobility of the day, he was soon to advertise his business as the Wimbledon Horse, Carriage and Motor Company. The entrance to the yard has been built over to extend the property.

The Hand in Hand public house, Crooked Billet, *c.* 1922 and 2002. The pole for the pub sign has found an additional use as a support for a washing line, as the gentleman on the ladder repaints the sign. The pub first sold beer in 1877 and was taken over by Young & Co. in 1974. It won the *Evening Standard* Pub of the Year competition in 1982. The pub entrance is behind the young mothers with the pram in the modern view.

Southside, Wimbledon Common, in 1907 and 2002. In 1907 there was no need for a sign warning, 'Caution: Horses approaching in road' as most traffic in those days was horse-powered. The entrance to the Grange is on the right and the High Street is straight ahead. Cows, sheep, horses and thousands of walkers kept the grass short up to the First World War but it is now allowed to grow knee-deep in places.

The High Street from Southside, Wimbledon Common, 1907 and 2002. Lingfield Road is to the right with The Green on the left. The scene is easily recognisable today: the only major changes have been the introduction of a one-way traffic system and the proliferation of street signs.

The High Street, facing north from the Dog and Fox public house, 1907 and 2002. Allington Close is to the left. The modern view is little altered from the 1907 scene except for the type of merchandise sold from the shops. The elegant turreted building further along the High Street was Thomas Mason's grocers and post office. It has been replaced with a modern five-storey block that hardly blends in with its neighbours in the old village.

The High Street, 1907 and 2002. In the background is the Dog and Fox public house. The pub is first mentioned in 1617 but the present building dates from 1869. The Georgian houses on the right are now home to restaurants and estate agents.

The High Street, facing north from the junction with The Ridgway, 1907 and 2002. The little bakery of A. Standen (left) is now the Wimbledon Village Bakery. On Saturday 15 June 2002 the England football team had just beaten Denmark in the World Cup tournament and crowds had gathered to celebrate outside the Pitcher and Piano public house on the left. A few football fans had gathered on the small traffic roundabout in the roadway, the original site of the Toynbee Fountain *(see opposite)*.

The magnificent bank building on the corner of the High Street and Belvedere Grove was built in about 1906 for the London & County Bank. The National Westminster Bank is now in residence. The Toynbee Fountain (right) was erected in 1868 to commemorate Joseph Toynbee, a noted ear and throat specialist and a founder member of the Village Club, but also as a part of the local Temperance campaign staunchly supported by Canon Henry Haygarth, vicar of the parish church.

The Ridgway, *c.* 1908 and 2002. Lauriston Road is to the left and the forecourt of the Swan public house is on the right. The King of Denmark public house is somewhat hidden just beyond Thornton Road on the right. This small group of shops, a builders, post office, restaurant and pubs feels like a village in its own right, but it was only created in the 1860s.

The Ridgway, *c.* 1920 and 2002. Ridgway Gardens is on the right. The only significant change has been the provision of a shelter for bus passengers on the right.

Emmanuel Church, *c.* 1908 and 2002. In the modern view the church is hidden behind the trees on the right-hand corner of the Ridgway and Lingfield Road. The railings have been removed from the cottages on the left and replaced with a simple wooden fence.

Merton & Raynes Park

A tram of the London United Electric Tramway Co. passes the Raynes Park Hotel in 1907 – the year trams came to Raynes Park. The hotel, dating from the 1870s, was rebuilt in 1904 and is today called the Raynes Park Tavern. The Rayne family owned the West Barnes Estate until selling it in 1866 to Richard Garth. The London & South Western Railway Co. opened the railway line in 1838 but the station at Raynes Park was not built until 1871, funded by Richard Garth.

The London General Omnibus garage in the High Street, Merton, in the early 1920s appeared little different from today except for the removal of one of the brick piers from the entrance, allowing the bigger modern buses to negotiate the opening. The cottages alongside have lost their chimneys, no doubt owing to the installation of central heating, and the original windows with their glazing bars have been replaced by a more simple design. One wonders what a mother today would say of her young children attempting to float a model boat in the River Wandle!

Merton High Street, *c.* 1914 and 2002. On the left in the earlier view is the eighteenth-century King's Head public house, which was rebuilt, enlarged and set back from the pavement in 1931. The Wandle was famous for the number of its watermills; on the right stood the Merton Board Mill, which was removed in the 1970s and replaced by a large shopping complex called the Savacentre.

The small parade of shops in Merton High Street near Grove Road had a mix of confectionery and newsagent's outlets in 1914. They have all closed. The corner shop is boarded up and looking rather sad. On the left of the 1914 photographer, not in view, stood a roller-skating rink that was later to be transformed into the Wimbledon Palais de Dance dance hall; a favourite venue for many years, it was sadly demolished in about 1999.

Merton High Street, viewed from Nelson Road looking west, *c.* 1930 and 2000. The building on the corner of Pincott Road housed a company which manufactured boxes and paper bags. The parade of shops included several undertakers and a Hope Mission Room. All this has been swept away except for the postbox. The High Path Housing Estate Residents' Association erected two replicas of cattle and horse troughs, on either side of Pincott Road, in January 2000 to celebrate the forthcoming new millennium.

Merton High Street, facing west, from outside the Nelson public house, 1912 and 2002. The two cars are turning into Haydons Road on the right. The modern view has changed little from the 1912 scene except for the change in goods sold from the shops and small details such as the stone capping missing from the roofline of the second block of shops.

The junction of Merton High Street and Merton Road, *c.* 1922 and 2002. The small parade of shops on the right, beyond the Horse & Groom public house, were demolished to make way for the High Path housing estate. F.T. Bowen's chemist's shop is now a Dallas fast-food outlet. The large building on the right was soon to be demolished for construction of South Wimbledon Underground station.

South Wimbledon Underground station on the corner of Merton High Street and Morden Road, *c.* 1936 and 2002. The station has altered very little. The traffic light system had only just been introduced in 1936 and the policeman on the corner is keeping a wary eye out for any indiscretions.

Kingston Road, Merton, *c.* 1925 and 2002. William Wood's off-licence, on the corner of Russel Road (right), is now C. James & Co. estate agents. The major loss here was the demolition of Rutlish School in the 1970s. This had stood since 1895 on the corner of Station Road, now Rutlish Road, where the large trees are in the modern view.

Kingston Road, Merton, 1907 and 2002. Rutlish School can be seen alongside the two carts on the left. The small finials and stone ball decorations on the roof parapets have given way to loft extensions providing a third floor, and the shop awnings have been dispensed with.

The level crossing on Kingston Road was first installed in 1855 and traffic had to be halted as each train arrived. The railway line was out of use for several years in the 1990s but came back to life on 31 May 2000 with the modernisation of the Wimbledon to Croydon Tramlink. The old gates have gone and the crossing is now controlled with traffic lights.

Coombe Lane, Raynes Park, *c.* 1908 and 2002. The London and South Western Bank is now a branch of Barclays and the forecourt of the Raynes Park Tavern has been built on, narrowing the pavement. A most dangerous cycle lane has been added to the streetscape. Pedestrians have great difficulty in boarding buses anywhere along Coombe Lane and other vehicles cannot stop where the cycle lane has been sited.

Author's Note

Patrick Loobey was born in 1947 and has lived in South London for most of his life. He joined the Wandsworth Historical Society (founded in 1953) in 1969 and has served on its archaeological, publishing and management committees, serving as chairman from 1991 to 1994 and 1998 to 2001. Having acquired Edwardian postcards of Wandsworth Borough and the surrounding area over thirty years, he has a wide-ranging collection encompassing many local roads and subjects. *Wimbledon Past & Present* complements the already substantial and ever-increasing number of Patrick's books.

The captions to the photographs in this book are but a brief glimpse into the varied and complex history of the area. For those seeking further information, the Wimbledon Society (formerly the John Evelyn Society) has published many books on the area's history and maintains a museum and archive on the Ridgway (open Saturdays). The Wandsworth Historical Society has also published histories that cover part of Wimbledon's past, namely Wimbledon Common, Southfields and Wimbledon Park. It can be contacted via the Wandsworth Museum, The Old Courthouse, Garratt Lane, Wandsworth. The Lawn Tennis Museum, Church Road, has an extensive library that can be consulted by appointment. The Windmill Museum, Wimbledon Common, should be contacted for details of opening times. The reference libraries at Crown House, Morden, and Hill Road, Wimbledon, have a wealth of material including early newspapers, deeds, directories, maps and parish records which are made available to those researching names, dates and addresses of families or business concerns.